MAKING HIS

Alan Baxter

Making History: My Life as a Scottish Metal Detectorist by Alan Baxter.

First edition published in Great Britain in 2024 by Extremis Publishing Ltd., Suite 218, Castle House, 1 Baker Street, Stirling, FK8 1AL, United Kingdom.
www.extremispublishing.com

Extremis Publishing is a Private Limited Company registered in Scotland (SC509983) whose Registered Office is Suite 218, Castle House, 1 Baker Street, Stirling, FK8 1AL, United Kingdom.

A CIP catalogue record for this book is available from the British Library.

ISBN: 978-1-7394845-4-5

Typeset in Sorts Mill Goudy, designed by The League of Moveable Type.

Printed and bound in Great Britain by IngramSpark, Chapter House, Pitfield, Kiln Farm, Milton Keynes, MK11 3LW, United Kingdom.

Cover artwork is Copyright © Alan Baxter, and is reproduced by kind permission of the copyright holder.

Cover design and book design is Copyright © Thomas A. Christie.

Internal photographic images are sourced from the author's private collection, with the exception of those stated in the Image Credits section which forms an extension to this legal page. The Treasure Trove Scotland reports referred to in this book are © Crown Copyright, and are reproduced by kind permission of the Treasure Trove Unit.

The copyrights of third parties are reserved. All third party imagery is used under the provision of Fair Use for the purposes of commentary and criticism. While every reasonable effort has been made to contact copyright holders and secure permission for all images reproduced in this work, we offer apologies for any instances in which this was not possible and for any inadvertent omissions.

MAKING HISTORY

My Life as a Scottish Metal Detectorist

Alan Baxter

EXTREMIS publishing

Foreword

It is with great pleasure that I recommend this book to the reader. The hobby of metal detecting has many participants from all walks of life. They range from the isolated individual who operates solo, to those who congregate in groups; from the occasional seeker who ventures out infrequently, to the obsessed who spend as much of their spare hours as possible roaming the countryside. They are all driven by the urge to discover long lost associations with earlier periods—and the thrill of the chase. All contribute greatly to our understanding of the past and the material culture of previous generations, and all will find this book useful.

Alan reveals something of this passion, of the feeling of exhilaration occasioned by a chance discovery, and of the satisfaction in a job well done. He goes on to show that from that climactic moment of uncovering the relic the process continues with the analysis and research into its character. This is a different state of mind, but no less rewarding a feeling. And imperceptibly, by dint of repetition and variety, it leads to an accumulation of knowledge and skill of which Alan is justly proud. I have gladly witnessed the development of his considerable expertise in numismatics, and in particular with the coinage of the Scottish realm.

Alan enthusiastically captures the nature of the hunt: the closeness and intimacy of the search when conducted alongside like-minded individuals; the hard slog involved in covering huge areas of terrain in variable weather conditions; the human contact and interaction with those on the fringes—the landowner, museum staff, dog walkers, farmers, and a myriad of others. Unearthing unseen artefacts from the bowels of the earth may be the pinnacle of the day, but it is preceded and followed by other special moments.

Alan also exemplifies the close co-operation needed between metal detectorists and the specialists in the form of numismatists, archaeologists, metallurgists, conservators, finds experts and the like. Here the procedures that he enumerates are vital—the recording of the location, the stratigraphy, the way in which an object is cleaned (or not), the reporting, the bureaucratic finds disposal process, to name just a few that you will find in the main text.

All of this results in a rich inheritance for posterity. On a simple level, this may take the form of a fascinating museum display with the finder's name attached. However, this serves to promote the hobby and its vital links with such institutions. It enables further research into typologies, distribution patterns, and cultural meaning. And in all of these Alan has been, and still is, very helpful.

Geoff Bailey
Archaeologist
March 2023

Contents

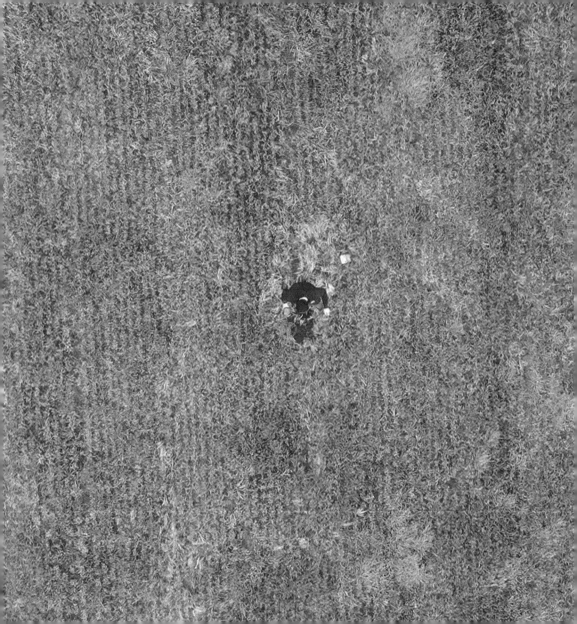

MAKING HISTORY

Alan Baxter

Introduction

Let me begin by introducing myself. My name is Alan Baxter, and I live in central Scotland where I have lived all my life. Around 12 years ago, I decided I needed a new direction in life. This was when my passion for metal detecting was born. Some might call it a mid-life crisis, but at a ripe youngish age of 31, and with a toddler and new baby at my feet—whilst working 12-hour shifts—I prefer to use the good old Scottish term, 'Freedom!'

It was my father who first introduced me to this fascinating hobby, and—with many treasures yet to be unearthed—I hope I can inspire others to become responsible detectorists too. In this book, I will guide you on how to gain some good permissions/land, whilst sharing the various research tools I frequently use and also explaining 'field walking'. If this alone doesn't inspire you, I will also be sharing with you some of the most remarkable finds my father and I have discovered in bonny Scotland over the last 12 years.

With the added benefits of exercise, walking out in the open air with breathtaking scenery and land steeped in history is great for the mind and soul. The excitement and highs you reach from the first suggested treasure tones of the detector will fill your blood with an addiction for more. This is an amazing hobby that gives back far more than it costs to do. You'll also find plenty of forums you can join online, connecting you to this elite group of like-minded people, and I would encourage you to join in some of the annual rallies where you can detect amongst others and build great friendships.

Starting the Hobby

There are a few things that you must consider when you make the decision that you are going to metal detect as a hobby. There are also a few rules and regulations that must be followed, and I have some good 'housekeeping' tips for when detecting in fields to keep you on the right side of the landowner, ensuring you get many happy years on your permission site.

The first thing you're going to need to do is purchase a metal detector. There is a huge range of them to choose from on the market. A decent metal detector can set you back by approximately £500, with the higher spec models reaching well over £1,000. You may be able to pick up a second-hand model from sellers on Internet forums or even other metal-detecting friends, but I would recommend you only buy from a trusted seller or site and—where possible—if you can, trial the metal detector first.

My current metal detector is a high-end model costing around £1,800. It is a heavy piece of equipment, but I love the smooth tones it sings. I've been using this detector for 8 years now and, hand on heart, I can honestly say I understand where this detector tells me to dig better than I understand the conversations I have at home with my partner. Each detector comes with its own built-in programs—you tend to find yourself swapping to different programs depending on the ecosystem you're operating within.

Do your research on your machines to find out which one will work best for you. If this is your first time going into the hobby, I would also suggest buying a detector on the lower pricing end of the market; this will allow you to get a feel for the hobby without investing too much too soon, then perhaps realising the hobby wasn't for you after all. For some, meeting like-minded people in group digs and getting out and about in the fresh air and countryside is just as important as the constant hunt for finds. You will get used to your machine over time and can pick up new programs to try on your detector either online or from detecting forums.

Over time you will adapt to the different tones of your detector and become so familiar with these tones that you might not even have to look at your detecting screen to know very roughly what's beneath your feet. On my metal detector, for example, a low tone is usually a thinner target object and could suggest you are on hammered coin territory. A high tone is usually a thicker object such as a big Georgian/Victorian penny or a tin can. These signals should be repeatable, i.e. when you sweep your detector one way across the target, the tone should be the same when sweeping it over the target at right angles. Throughout this book, I will be talking about my specific metal detector and how it reacts to different metallic targets, but it must be noted these are the tones/repeatability I expect from my metal detector/program and will differ from metal detector to metal detector and program to program that are built into, or manually inserted into, the metal detector. For example, a thinner target object on another program/metal detector might give the opposite tone from my detector; it could be a high tone. Sometimes you can get a tone one way and not the other. This means the coin or artefact may be on its side.

With experience I've learned to avoid iron tones unless detecting on a battle site, mainly because—more times than not—it's just junk in the soil below. These signals on my machine are high again but are not repeatable and are more scratchy tones. This is a common issue found amongst beginners starting the hobby; they can dig iron all day and waste their time. If you can master this, you have cracked it.

Whilst you're researching your next purchase, you should consider getting some form of insurance for metal detecting. This is optional, and it is simply a form of public liability insurance. Having this cover can also help persuade landowners to grant you permission to detect on their land.

Now let's discuss some rules and regulations. You simply cannot and must never detect on scheduled monument sites. These are sites that are legally protected due to their historical/archaeological importance. A good example of such a site, and there are lots, would be the Antonine Wall. Detecting on these sites is against the law and will land you in deep trouble. Whilst some scheduled sites are obvious, others are not. There are many useful online tools; I am not familiar with the website tools used for England, but for Scottish detecting, I am an avid user of the website called Pastmap. This is a fantastic website that details where sites of historical importance are located within Scotland, and gives information about where artefacts have been found in the past through metal detecting and field-walking, etc. There are various functions and views that you can use on the maps. My own preferred functions are the 'Scheduled' and the 'Canmore' icons/views.

The Scheduled icon/view is a good one to use, as it shows you exactly what it states. You can find out where all the scheduled monuments are, such as: Roman forts; castles; historic settlements, etc. Using this view on the maps will highlight, in red, the area and boundaries of these scheduled monuments. If in doubt, look up the website at *https://pastmap.org.uk*. There are other useful online tools and websites you can use that will clarify the law of scheduled monuments and where to find them, I would encourage anyone to use these to keep themselves right. As mentioned already, you must never detect on these sites. The purpose of using this view for me is to give a good indication that there was historical activity within the area being researched.

The Canmore view will show you if there are any metal detecting/field-walking finds in the area or any medieval plough areas (rig and furrow).

Another website I frequently visit is that of the National Library of Scotland. There is an option on this site called 'Side-by-Side'. This option will present a split-screen view where you can then explore the current map of Scotland alongside a historical map. One of the oldest maps you can display is Roy's map of the 1740s/50s. I use this to find out where historic villages and buildings were located. It also helps me pinpoint areas to avoid. Here is a link to the website: *https://maps.nls.uk*

Another rule I always follow is to respect the land you are detecting on. This includes filling in all of your holes properly. Failure to do so could result in injury to livestock and damage to machinery. You must also make sure you take all your rubbish home; this includes any junk metal you find. It's good practice to collect junk metal such as lead and copper and recycle these. Big lumps of iron left at the side of holes can be harmful to farm machinery, so the message is very simple: 'take all rubbish home—domestic and metal finds.'

The final of these important rules to follow is the one on ensuring all gates are closed behind you. I have had my own personal experience of this one. When entering a field with a gate, I will always double-check that the gate has been closed securely behind me. Failure to adhere to this rule runs the risk of livestock escaping out onto roads and causing road blockages or accidents. There is no greater way to annoy the landowner and to lose your detecting permission.

As mentioned above, I have had my own personal experience of this issue. My father and I were returning from just another normal day of detecting. As we made our way back to our car, we realised that one of the gates was 'missing'. It quickly became apparent that someone had stolen the gate, and the sheep had escaped and were now running around everywhere! It was simply chaos. I immediately called the farmer, and the situation was brought under control, earning my father and I a few extra brownie points for sticking around and helping. It just goes to show the lengths criminals will go to, to be stealing gates in broad daylight!

I also would never walk on land that has just been freshly seeded with food crops or grass, unless you have permission from the landowner to do so. I would wait until the crops have been harvested. All of these rules and regulations help to safeguard the land, habitats, and its inhabitants. If you choose not to follow these, this could result in you losing a good permission or worse.

As a final suggestion, prior to seeking authority to proceed with detecting from a landowner, it may be worthwhile taking a walk across fields that have been freshly ploughed. A ploughed field can unearth a range of materials, and I will always be on the lookout for any Roman and medieval pottery. Roman pottery varies in textures and styles, but the most obvious and common type of Roman pottery is 'samian ware'. You can identify these pieces of pottery by the orange-glazed shiny surface. These pots and dishes were of high status and mostly made in Gaul (modern-day France).

When searching for medieval pottery, the most common find in Scotland is a type of pot called 'white gritty ware'. This is 12th-15th century AD pottery and can be described as its name suggests; white/cream in colour with the texture of a dog biscuit. This type of pottery was mainly made at kiln sites throughout southern and eastern Scotland.

The best time to check out a ploughed field is after a period of rainfall. This helps to wash the dirt off the surface of the pottery and expose it. Sometimes, however, pottery works its way into fields from manure being brought onto the fields from outside locations. This may create the illusion that there was Roman or medieval activity on the site, but in fact, it is not a natural find for that field. This has been a successful method for me in the past, and I continue to look for the areas with a high intensity of pottery and start detecting them.

Once you have located an area that's of interest to you, you must seek the landowner's permission to detect on their land. It is helpful to have a few options, as not all landowners will allow you onto their property. You must be prepared to go out knocking on some doors. Making yourself smart and presentable helps, and always try to keep a polite and friendly tone. Your aim is to sell the hobby for all its benefits, whilst instilling the landowner with confidence that you are responsible, respectful, and will always abide by their conditions. If you've done a bit of detecting previously, building a portfolio of your finds that you can display can also help gain you permission, as this shows experience. If the landowner refuses you permission, I wouldn't pursue this any further; move on to your next option. You will eventually get a permission to detect on. When seeking an agreement to metal detect on a landowner's property, it is important to also reach an agreement on any financial settlements for finds—i.e. the *ex-gratia* rewards. This agreement is entirely between you and the landowner; in my opinion, a 50/50 split would be a fair outcome. You will be out in all conditions and will have the tools and equipment, but without the land, there won't be any finds.

In Scotland, all man-made finds must be reported by law to Treasure Trove Scotland. There are exceptions to this, such as not having to report modern coins or modern ceramics, and you can find more information on their website: *http://treasuretrovescotland.co.uk*. They will decide the outcome of whether these finds should be claimed and allocated to a museum in Scotland, or disclaimed and handed back to the finder. Natural finds such as fossils do not fall under the categories you are required to report to the Treasure Trove. I would recommend you always look on the Treasure Trove website to keep up to date with the latest information and legislation. In the beginning I would take everything I found through to the National Museum of Scotland. I have since learned, over the years, what should and should not be recorded. Most of this learning came from the advice and guidance I received from the very kind and resourceful Treasure Trove officers. Not only were they patient and understanding of my many questions, but they also really helped embed the process of reporting finds. When reporting my own finds, I will send an email with a picture of my finds next to a scale or modern coin, along with the grid reference of the find site. It is then up to Treasure Trove Scotland whether they wish to claim or disclaim the find. You will receive a disclaimer certificate for anything not claimed. If they choose to claim the find, however, you must submit it to them (this usually involves a trip for me through to the National Museum in Edinburgh), and you will receive a finder's certificate along with an *ex-gratia* reward. This process can take several weeks/months. Sometimes significant finds will go on display in museums. There is nothing more rewarding, in my opinion, than being able to visit your own personal finds, seeing your name next to them in the cabinets, and knowing you contributed to finding a rich piece of history that can now be shared with others all over the world.

Another way of finding land to detect on is to join a metal detecting group. There are multiple groups you can find and join online. In these groups, you will find regular 'rallies' (bigger group digs) which are organised that you can sign up to. You may even be fortunate enough to be invited on to other members' permission sites.

When you have a site to detect on, and you want to make sure you cover all your ground, I find it helpful to take canes out with me to use as guides. I use them to set up boxes; this method gives me greater confidence knowing I'm sweeping every inch of the field and gives me a greater prospect of finding 'the old gear,' as I like to call it.

Finds and
My Permissions

Falkirk

The first ever permission I gained was in 2012 in Falkirk District. This area is steeped in history, especially Roman history, with some important hoards and artefacts coming from the area.

I remember going out to do my first search. It was a bleak, cold January morning, made even more dreich by the damp mist that swirled in the air clinging to every inch of its surroundings. Dressed in warm attire, I set up my metal detector and went to work. I was detecting for a good couple of hours and was already feeling quite happy with myself after finding some musket balls, when my detector let out a signal indicating I needed to dig. It was here I unearthed my first ever Roman silver denarius of Nerva (reigned AD 96–98).

I was over the moon. This was a great first find and a rare one at that to discover in Scotland. When I dug it out of the soil, at first I had no idea what it was, other than it was shaped like a coin and was black. I knew though that it had to be old. I was so excited and impatient to find out what I had, I got out my phone and called my dad who drove down to meet me. I saw him coming out of the mist; he took a look at the coin, and he said, 'I think that's Roman, son.' From that moment on, I was hooked.

The feeling you get from finding something so old is amazing! When the realisation hits you that you're the first person to touch the coin for 2000 years, it brings about new questions. Who lost this? How was it lost? It's just fascinating. The knowledge you gain over the years regarding coinage and artefacts is incredible. You develop a natural thirst to learn as much as you can and remember it. I can now ID most coinage with a specialist's knowledge of early Roman and medieval coins, and artefacts from the same period. Even my dad has become a bit of a historian on these subject matters. If only our history teachers could see us now!

The longer this hobby takes hold, the more experienced you become with history, geography, farming, and artefacts. I wasn't always the knowledgeable person I am today. Back at the beginning, a few years after that Nerva Roman coin find, my dad and I were out detecting when we stumbled across a green-coloured artefact. Between us, we both concluded that the find was just an old Victorian door handle, so my dad took it home and put it in an old sweet tin along with the rest of his old tatty Victorian coins and artefacts. For a while it sat in the old tin until, one day, I took it through to the National Museum of Scotland along with a medieval seal. I took a lot of obscure artefacts across to the Museum in the early days as I just wasn't 100% sure about them, and the Treasure Trove officers were really accommodating at detailing the history. I decided to take the handle through to have it confirmed as being Victorian. I took the train through that day with my daughter, who was 4 years old at the time, and I was greeted by one of the Treasure Trove officers. The officer took my finds off me and looked at the handle and said, 'I will have to show this to the Iron Age specialist. There's something about its style; could be old.' She wasn't 100% sure.

I had only just boarded the train, ready to head back home, when I got a phone call which I will never forget. It was the officer I had met earlier that day, and she told me that the

Iron Age specialist had gotten back to her, and he confirmed that what I had thought was a Victorian handle was actually a very fine example of a rare Iron Age copper alloy tankard handle dating to approximately 2000 years ago. Upon hearing this, I uttered a few words in my complete shock, and at that point, my daughter called out 'daddy' and swiftly brought me back to reality as people looked around at me on the train. My head was absolutely buzzing! I was completely blown away—and it just goes to show that you should always check and try to research your finds, as you never know what you have. If ever in doubt, drop the Treasure Trove an e-mail.

This was an amazing find. It was complete and in good condition. The handle would have been attached to a wooden vessel for ale. It was not like your

modern-day drink handle for putting your hand in; it was too small for this. I think its purpose would have probably been to hang the wooden vessel up in a roundhouse, as you would do with a kitchen utensil. The traces of leather can still be seen where the handle attached to the vessel.

After this discovery, my father and I then, of course, went back to the same area where the tankard handle had been found. It was another misty morning, and we started detecting at first light as we mostly tend to do. The area we were detecting was beautiful, with stunning surroundings. Not much has changed over the centuries, and we are fortunate to be able to observe the amazing views of the Ochil Hills. There are normally roe deer that venture out from the woods and into the open field, but they dart back into the woods when they catch sight of us. I was really excited as to what the day would bring.

I was detecting for around an hour when I got a loud signal! I dug down approximately 8 inches and out came a copper alloy terret ring. I immediately knew it was Iron Age, and the condition of it was remarkable. I was ecstatic with this find! Terret rings were used as reign guides for horse-pulled chariots and would have been attached to a wooden yoke that would have gone round two of the horses' backs. I took the terret ring through to the National Museum of Scotland and, on this occasion, I received the VIP treatment. I was invited into the heart of the Museum; the staff were blown away by the find. I clearly remember the smile on the museum curator's face when he saw the terret ring and examined it under the microscope. The terret dates from around 50 BC based on typology.

This elaborate high-status terret ring also turned out to be one of the best found in Scotland due to its decorative enamel. I can only describe it as 'simply stunning,' with its red and yellow enamelled cells and red dots on each endpoint or lug. In its day, it would have looked spectacular, with the shiny gold-coloured copper glinting in the sunlight, as the chariot passed by... amazing!

Both these finds can currently be viewed in Callendar House, Falkirk, with my name against them in the Roman Gallery. The display itself was set up by my friend, the Falkirk Archaeologist Geoff Bailey.

Whilst visiting the National Museum of Scotland and handing in the terret ring, the museum curator of Prehistoric and Roman Archaeology declared they would visit the site and then arrange for an excavation to take place. I was surprised to be asked what day suited me to hold an excavation on the site. I was thrilled and felt very humbled that they were including me in this historic moment.

The museum curator of Prehistoric and Roman Archaeology and the museum archaeologists came to the site in April 2015. An earth-digging machine was funded to scrape back the area where the tankard handle and terret ring were discovered. They believed the artefacts were intentionally put in the ground as votive offerings.

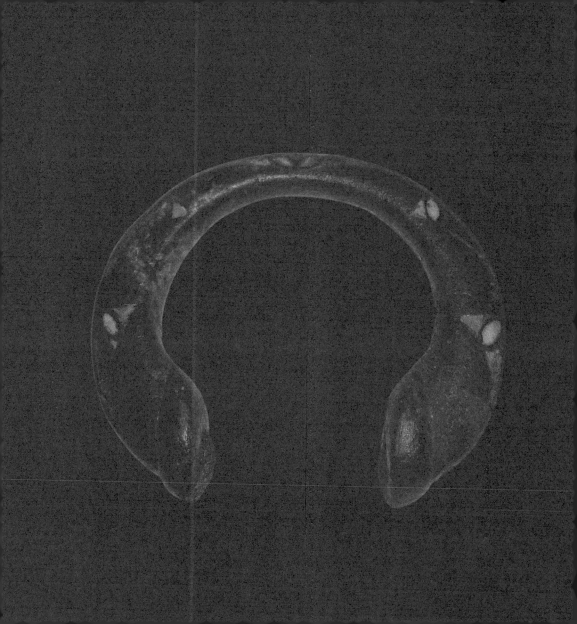

I remember being ablaze with excitement and eager to see what the day would bring. We all met on site, with my dad and another friend joining us to help further detect the area. Roughly 3 acres of the land were marked out with orange spray paint and then the machine was set to work, taking off 10-inch spits of earth. We would then detect this and mark the locations of new signals with a white marker flag. The archaeologists would then excavate the signals.

We all worked together as a team. Once we hit about 2 feet down, and a few Victorian pennies/tin cans later, my dad got a good high-tone signal. We pinned it with a white flag, and an archaeologist came over to dig. We all had a gut feeling we had struck something remarkable.

After about 5 minutes of careful digging, the top of an *in situ* plain copper alloy terret ring was exposed. Almost instantaneously, the archaeologists knew it was an Iron Age object. They began to slow down the exposure of this terret ring, taking a pencil drawing of the terret half exposed and lots of pictures at different angles. I had never seen anything like this, and it was a unique experience to observe them doing their job with such care and professionalism. The pencil drawing was amazing and looked like an actual photo.

After about 2 hours—yes, 2 hours—they got the terret ring out of the ground. I was grateful for the opportunity to hold the terret ring before it was placed into a storage box. I was over the moon; a copper alloy Roman trumpet brooch from around AD 150 was also discovered just outside the excavation area. 'The combination of these artefacts makes them the most significant metallic find since 1933 in Falkirk District' (Falkirk Archaeologist Geoff Bailey, personal communication, December 5, 2023).

On that previous occasion, over 2,000 Roman silver denarii were found at the old Falkirk Bus Station.

Over the next two years, on the same field outside of the Iron Age hoard area, a copper alloy Iron Age linch-pin was found. This would have been found on a chariot wheel and would have been used to keep the Chariot Wheel locked on, much like a modern-day car bolt. This was another very rare find for Scotland. You can see the copper terminal with two decorative lines going around it, with a paddle-shaped finger grip, and the iron terminal for locking inside the chariot wheel.

A few medieval silver coins of King Edward I (reigned AD 1272–1307) and II (reigned AD 1307–1327) were also found. It was nice to find these hammered coins in the same field as the Iron Age material. It shows the importance of the site

and its continuous occupation from the Iron Age through to the medieval period.

The coin shown on the top left of the opposite page is a Berwick mint; the next 3 are London mint, and the bottom left is a Canterbury mint. The next is Durham, and with the bottom two on the far right, the mint is blundered.

To give a basic overview of these Edward I/II pennies, they mostly weigh 1.2-1.4 grams each. The obverse legend reads in Latin: +EDW REX ANGL DNS HYB, which translates to Edward King of England and Lord of Ireland. The reverse reads (and for an example, I will take the most common Edward I mint, London): CIVI/TAS/LON/DON which translates to the City of London.

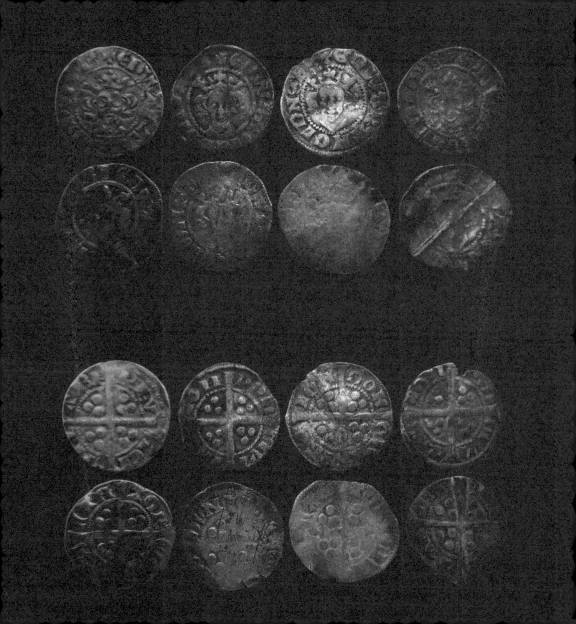

West Lothian

In 2013 I gained a new permission in West Lothian, Scotland. I was also able to renew my original permission in Falkirk District. Having two permissions meant my father and I had more options on which land to detect.

It was in West Lothian that we found a Papal bulla. Part of the Treasure Trove report written by Stuart Campbell (CO.TT. 101/14) that was used to describe this Papal bulla is as follows: 'A Papal bulla, the name of the issuing Pope now obscured, the two lines of text with the name now reduced to simply last letters of 'o' and 's' with the last line PP IIII indicating that the issuer was the fourth of that name. The other side has the standard reverse of all papal bulla showing the heads of St Peter and of St Paul under the abbreviated title 'SPASPE' (Sanctus PAulus and Sanctus PEtrus)' (Stuart Campbell CO.TT. 101/14).

It was exploring the same site that led to the discovery of a Bronze Age axehead. The axe was found a good 12 inches deep into the soil. This is usual for an object of this size; bigger objects can be found at depth. The signal tone from the detector was extremely loud and high-pitched. I remember that signal to this day. The tone nearly blew my ears off. It was clear from the onset with a signal like this that the find was to be of considerable size. I remember taking the object out of the ground and my dad saying: 'That looks like an axe.' It was not iron this time, but bronze. We knew from that moment it had to be ancient—around 4000 years old.

We have never found a Bronze Age axe again—and, if you think of the size of the population back then, it's no wonder. A small post-medieval toy hammer was also found on this site, and some of these finds can be viewed in the Linlithgow Museum.

Part of the Treasure Trove report written by Dr Natasha Ferguson (CO.TT. 146/13) that was used to describe this axehead is as follows: 'Middle Bronze Age flanged axehead with pronounced butt. The flange tips are also curved in towards the centre. Behind the butt is an oval shaped facet with gently sloping sides. Although there is some surface loss due to corrosion the general condition is good with little sign of wear. The findspot is interesting as it is located between two prehistoric standing stones and in an area of land drained in the 18th century. The close proximity of the axehead to a wetland area, and its generally good condition, may suggest ritual deposit rather than loss' (Dr Natasha Ferguson CO.TT. 146/13).

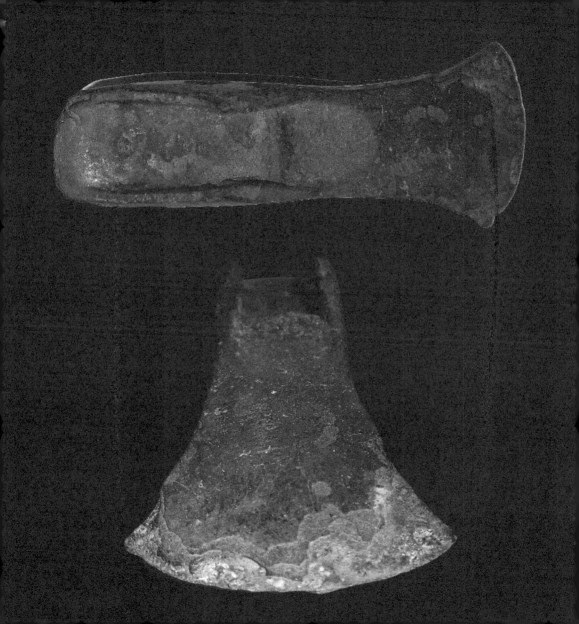

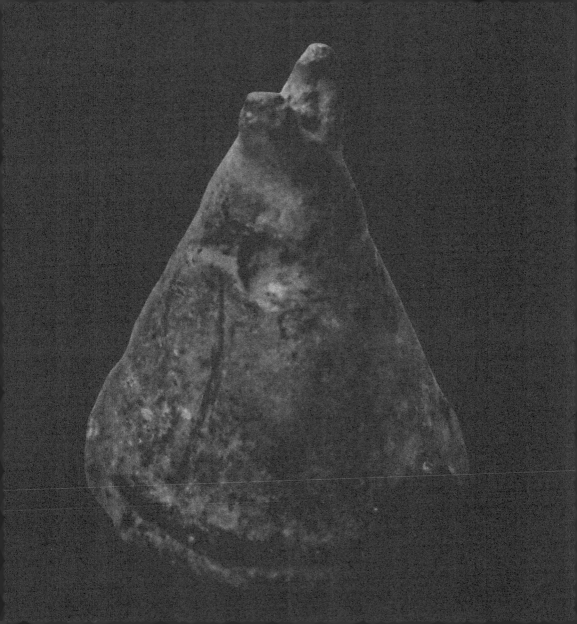

Midlothian

In 2015, I gained a further two permissions in Midlothian. One of the permissions was on an impressive castle site, where I found two medieval horse harness pendants. One was a *fleur de lis* design, while the other was a bell-shaped harness. These would have been worn as decoration around the horse's chest. Both of these pendants were found right next to the castle wall, which accords with the theory that you need to be close to—or on top of—a historical site and activity.

My other permission was near a medieval village and a Roman road in Midlothian. I remember this site was all pasture, and it was 1,200 metres above sea level. It was freezing during the winter and even with my jacket, hat, and gloves on, my hands and my lips were so cold, that they would turn a definite shade of blue. Despite the bone-chilling conditions, the will to find the 'old gear' was too much, and it was this obsession that motivated me to go on. There were a couple of occasions when my father and I had to quit; the ground was just too solid from the frost—we simply couldn't get a spade in the ground.

I found a silver Roman denarius on this site dating to the time of Trajan (reigned AD 98-117). I also found a copper alloy Roman handle.

Part of the Treasure Trove report written by Dr. Fraser Hunter (CO.TT. 90/15) that was used to describe this Roman handle is as follows: 'Roman copper-alloy handle from an item of furniture or a vehicle. Concave-sided handle with apparently flat base and concave top with central protruding boss. Much of the original surface is lost but there are vestigial traces of a double-incised line of lathe-turned decoration on the upper surface. The piece is worn, with one edge of the top broken. The attachment tang is concealed in a mass of iron corrosion. H 26.6 mm overall; D 24 mm' (Dr. Fraser Hunter CO.TT. 90/15).

I remember, due to the weather, finding the next item. It was raining so hard that the hole I was digging was filling up fast with water. The object was

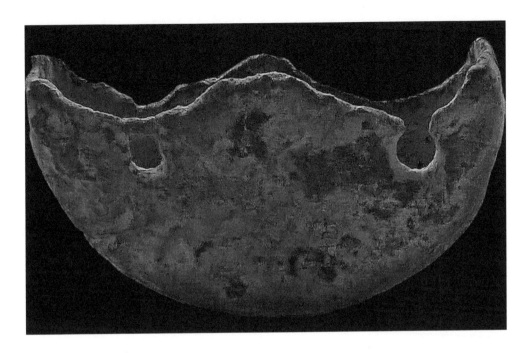

buried a good 15 inches down, and my arm was soaking as I lifted it out of the hole. I had uncovered a copper alloy Roman scabbard chape! Part of the Treasure Trove report written by Dr Fraser Hunter (CO.TT. 12/16) that was used to describe this artefact is as follows: 'Roman copper-alloy scabbard chape; the form is typical of the second century, and in a Scottish context this suggests an Antonine date. The findspot suggests it was a casual loss from troops moving along Dere St.' (Dr Fraser Hunter CO.TT. 12/16).

The final object I found on this site was a small square copper belt mount covered with silver. Part of the Treasure Trove report written by Stuart Campbell (CO.TT. 74/17) that was used to describe this mount is as follows.: 'Square sheet silver plate or mount recovered with a copper alloy plate that suggests it functioned as a strap end. The mount depicts what appears to be a dove and has been made by repousse (stamped out by a die from the rear) with the details of feather, legs and beak finished by engraving. The mount has also been gilded. Such mounts are rare survivals and dating is problematic, although the majority of such pictorial belt fittings tend to be c.1200 and depict (as this one does) imagery found on religious art. 15.5 x 16mm' (Stuart Campbell CO.TT. 74/17).

Fife

The most recent permission that I—along with my father—gained was a huge one. Thousands of acres of mainly arable land with a few pasture fields. It is a prime location in Fife surrounded by history. I was really excited to detect on this land, and I knew we had a good chance of finding the 'old gear' based on researching the maps and local history. What was to follow was nothing short of mind-blowing, and it exceeded all my expectations.

My father and I found around 500 items between us, mostly from one specific area/site within the permission, and they ranged from the Bronze Age to late medieval. I believe the site was undetected due to there being signals everywhere. Every 3 feet, I'd hear another signal from my detector. It was either an artefact of copper, lead, tin or a coin, with the occasional shotgun cartridge. Most of these finds were small, and the signal from my detector was a low tone. We were fortunate with the conditions of the field at the time. We were able to sweep our detectors close to the soil, making it easier for the signals to come through. The conditions must be right. Medium to high stubble on fields are not good conditions; you end up going right over the top of the targets.

My father and I had found what is believed to be a possible settlement or village. I will refer it to be as such throughout this book and—as one could expect—there was a honey spot in the centre of it. It probably had been occupied from around 1500 BC to AD 1470. I will take you through these man-made finds in order, from the earliest around to the latest from this settlement.

I was so lucky to find this piece of land! There was a great deal of research that went into finding the area and, due to the conditions of the land, the soil had shielded and been kind to the history it concealed for so long. It always amazes me to think that—long ago—people worked, lived, and died here. Times were hard, there was no running water, and food had to be hunted, foraged, or grown. There was no electricity, and the country was constantly at war. The plague would have ripped through the land, and the population had to battle with this on top of other diseases such as leprosy, making times tough indeed. There would have been a lot of hustle and bustle on market days, and now in its place there lies just empty barren fields. To me this is a very important site, and I'm proud it is on the map for Scottish history. I would love to go back in time and see what this site looked like at its peak! With each find unearthed, it brings us a new story and vision of how these times would have looked.

This site is where I discovered my oldest find—a non-metallic fossil fern. 'It was around 300 million years old, and was from a Lepidodendron tree of the

Carboniferous Period. It was a tree root that had rotted away, and the void had filled up with sand. This is mostly what the site is composed of, with the soil having a high sand ratio. Over time the sand solidified into sandstone and took up the form of the root with the pimples on the surface. It is basically the bark from the tree root, and the technical name for this is a fossil fern' (Falkirk

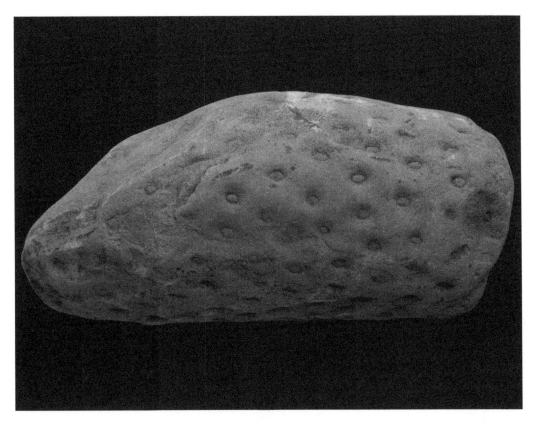

archaeologist Geoff Bailey, personal communication, December 5, 2023). Falkirk archaeologist Geoff Bailey passed this information on, as he collects these fossils. I am fortunate enough to have such friendships with various experts, as I'm by no means an expert in all fields. These types of finds don't come under the Scottish Treasure Trove Act because they are not man-made. Any non-metallic find is known as an 'eyes only' find, as you basically scope these items out with your sight. The piece I found was a nice specimen; it was big and perfectly formed. I was so pleased with it, and believe it to be a worthy inclusion in this book for the sheer fact of its age alone. You should always keep an eye out for these types of finds on the ground when you are detecting. You could stumble upon a nice flint arrowhead, as well as traces of medieval pottery, etc. (I have yet to find a flint arrowhead. Hopefully one day!)

The first metallic item is probably around 3500 years old. It is a possible Bronze Age copper alloy arrow tip. It is a pretty cool find due to the rarity of it. Usually, arrow tips were made from flint during the Stone Age and into the early part of the Bronze Age. This find shows the Bronze Age people evolving into the use of metal tools.

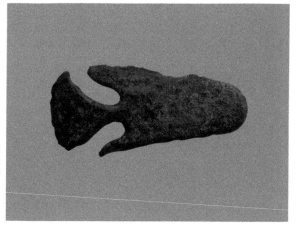

Two copper alloy roman trumpet brooches and one copper alloy loop fastener, both dated to around AD 100 to AD 200, and a copper alloy roman coin of Tacitus (reigned AD 275–276AD)—not a common coin for Scotland.

The next four finds are Roman and date from around AD 100 to AD 300. It was nice to find these on this site as I do like a bit of Roman and it shows the vast period of activity that existed in this area.

The next find is a lovely rare Roman copper-alloy openwork enamelled racquet-headed plate brooch. Part of the Treasure Trove report written by Dr. Fraser Hunter (CO.TT. 86/18) that was used to describe this brooch is as follows: 'Roman copper-alloy openwork enamelled plate; the hinged pin and catchplate are lost, as are parts of the terminal margins. The form is often termed a raquet-headed brooch. The body is a tapered openwork oval, its face enamelled with alternating opaque red and opaque mid-blue blocks with no field divisions. At the narrow end is a disc with three circular lobes,

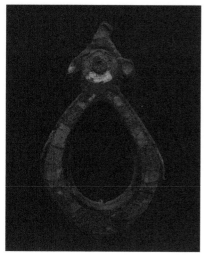

one with a surviving orange enamelled dot; between the lobes, the margin has decorative incisions. The disc has a circular enamelled field (D 7 mm) with a reserved circle, central ? blue dot, and outer field with four alternating opaque red and white blocks (again with no field divisions). The rear has been filed. H 37.8, W 22, T 7.8 mm. The form is typical of Roman plate brooches of the late second / early third century, most likely made in Gaul' (Dr. Fraser Hunter CO.TT. 86/18).

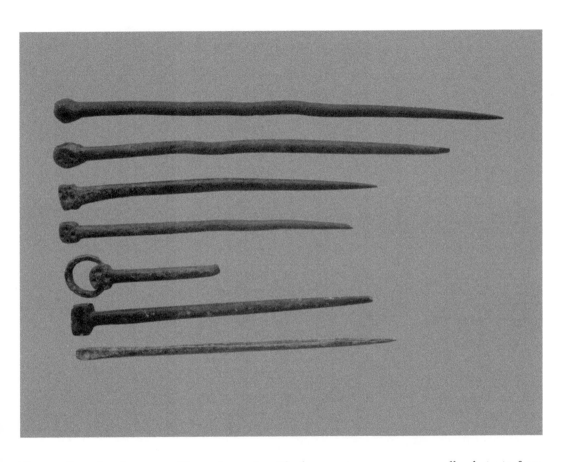

The top five pins shown are Norse dress pins. The bottom two are a copper alloy hairpin from same period and a medieval copper alloy needle, circa 12th century AD.

The next few artefacts are from around the 7th–11th century AD. The first set are five Norse copper alloy ringed pins, used to fasten cloaks, and again are rare to find in Scotland. To get so many on one site was truly astonishing.

This next object is a nice early medieval copper alloy stirrup mount, again with an intricate design. It has lots of swirls and is a lovely open-worked design. Another very rare find for Scotland. Unfortunately, part of it is broken.

The next find doesn't have a definite ID, but it is possibly an early medieval

copper alloy strap end in the shape of a Pictish fish with three dots. These are very rare to find.

Moving on, we have 12th–15th century AD artefacts and coinage. Based on the finds, you can determine that the settlement seems to have peaked around the late 13th century AD. This makes sense as after this period would have followed the Scottish Wars of Independence, famine, and plague. Then it would seem the population moved on around AD 1470 and the finds mirror this, which is very interesting.

I will start with the artefacts from this period and then move on to the coinage. The most interesting thing of note was that the dress accessories from England are identical to the finds from this site in the heart of Scotland. This tells us that the clothing and accessories were very similar throughout Scotland and England. First up are buckle finds. In the picture below they are all of copper alloy, and the condition of the patina on these is great. 39 were found in total, although the plough has managed to break one or two.

The buckles pictured are mainly from the 12th–15th century AD. There are two, however, that are from an earlier era. The buckle second from the bottom left is from the 11th century AD and has zoomorphic beasts coming from both terminals. The one next

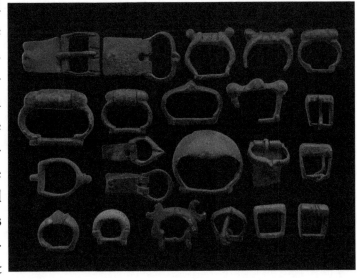

to this (to the right) has antler-type terminals which suggests it dates even earlier, and is possibly the oldest of these buckles. Apart from these two there are five common types of buckles from this site. There are oval framed buckles with rollers where the pins would meet in the centre, oval framed buckles with ornate outside edges, rectangular/square framed buckles and lastly d-framed buckles. Some of the buckles still have their plates attached. It's a very nice selection of different buckles in great condition.

The next set of finds has been grouped together. There are 42 copper alloy buckle plates that, at some point, have come free from their buckles. The sheer amount of those found gives us a good indication of how much activity there was on this site.

The next set of finds are copper alloy and are related to girdles or other straps. They are called strap loops, as they hold down loose parts of the strap. There are two main types of frames for these—oval frames and rectangular frames. 16 of these were found.

Next, we have 13 copper alloy strap-ends. These would have been attached to the very end of a belt strap. Some of the strap-ends that we found still had the

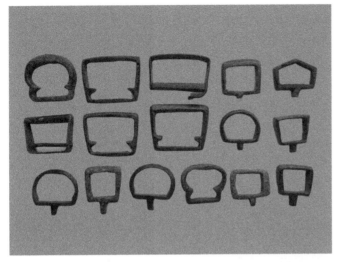

original leather inside of them. One of the strap-ends, as you will see from the picture, has a nice saltire type design.

Mounts were by far the most common find from this site. I found 95 in total, all of which were copper alloy. They were designed mostly for decoration on girdles/straps. The top two rows are mostly simple bar mounts, thin and rectangular shaped, with some displaying elaborate edges. These are the most common mounts out of the 95 found. The five mounts in the second row on the right side are bar mounts with central lobes that were crudely

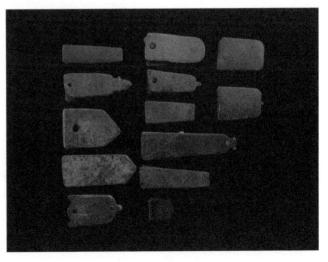

cross hatched. In the third row, you can see a mixture of cinquefoil/sexfoil and octofoil mounts with 5, 6 and 8 petalled flowers. The fourth row shows a group of mounts called polygonal domed mounts with central holes. Finally, the bottom 2 rows are a mixture of various types. There are arrow pendants, hook mounts, *fleur de lis* mounts, lozenge-shaped mounts and crescent shaped

mounts. The variety and condition of these mounts are just astounding.

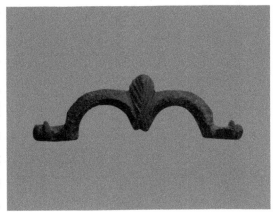

This next artefact is a copper alloy purse hanger. It would have been attached by the end terminals and would have been held on the strap by two bar mounts with pendant hooks. You can see there is a nice little flower petal design in the centre.

Moving away from buckle and strap related dress accessories, and on to something a bit different and ornate; finger rings are the next topic we will cover. From this great site, seven in all were found: five copper alloy rings and two silver rings. The silver one pictured on the following page is a silver gilt fede ring. There is an inscription around the hoop, and this is one of my better medieval higher status finds. I remember the day I found this artefact very well. I was detecting with one of my friends and it was a glorious sunny spring day in 2018. So far, I was having no success with any signals. Around 2–3 hours later I got a nice signal near a busy road at the edge of the field. I dug down thinking I would find a bottle top or tin can, as this is your most common find at the side of any busy road. I kept digging, and the first thing I could see was a silvery circle with soil in the centre.

My initial thoughts were that I had unearthed an aluminium juice bottle top. As I picked it up and wiped away the soil from the centre, I was expecting to find the usual details of a bottle top. However, as the soil fell through the middle, I instantly got a rush of adrenaline. There in front of me, before my very eyes was the writing on the side of a ring.

The more I revealed of the ring, the more excited I became. I knew straight away it was medieval and not only was it complete, but it also still had a silver shine to it. It was stunning as it glistened in the spring sunshine. I ran over to my friend and all I could say was 'Look! Look!" I picked him up and spun him around; I was feeling euphoric! It was an amazing feeling, and I will always remember that day for the rest of my life. Part of the Treasure Trove report written by Emily Freeman (CO.TT. 130/18) that was used to describe this medieval ring is as follows: 'A complete silver gilt fede ring with inscription around the hoop. The ring has been made from a thick silver strip (presumably cast) brazed into a circle with the details of the lettering and the clasped hands added by engraving and chiseling. The inscription

is set upon a series of raised squares with the letters set out as block capitals against a hatched background. Between each letter are raised rhombi with irregular diagonal engraved lines forming rough saltire crosses. The inscription reads "I h E S", an abbreviated form of "IHESUS NAZARENUS REX IOUDOREUM" or "Jesus of Nazareth, King of the Jews" which was commonly believed to protect the wearer from violent death and which can be paralleled on jewellery from hoards which date to c.1300. The ring is in very fine condition, although the gilding has mostly been lost. Fede rings were usually given as wedding or betrothal gifts, and many examples from Scotland have this same protective inscription' (Emily Freeman CO.TT. 130/18).

A lot of silver has gone into this ring— approximately eight medieval pennies, as the ring weighed 9.5g—and the cost of the craftsmanship and the gold plating would have put the price up by some amount. This ring would have been unaffordable for the normal medieval peasant, and would have belonged to someone with a much higher status. The ring is now on display at Kirkcaldy Galleries in Fife.

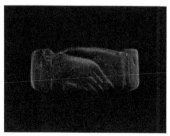

The next finger ring, out of the seven I'm going to mention from the site, is a copper alloy one. It is in great condition and has a nice silky copper patina. It is very similar to the aforementioned silver ring and is another fede ring. You can see this one has the

Wemyss Ware chamber pot, decorated with roses. Likely to have been painted by Edwin Sandland at the Fife Potter's, Kirkcaldy. (Top left.)

Wemyss Ware basket, decorated with dog roses. (Top right.)

Bronze Age copper axehead, dating from around 2150 to 1800 BC, and discovered through metal-detecting at ████████. Acquired through Treasure Trove, and funded with assistance of the National Fund for Acquisitions.

Medieval silver finger ring, dating from around 1300 AD and discovered through metal-detecting by Alan Baxter at ████. Acquired through Treasure Trove and funded with assistance of the National Fund for Acquisitions.

Commemorative teapot in Wemyss Ware style, made by Griselda Hill Pottery, Ceres, to mark the Golden Jubilee in 2002.

Wemyss Ware inkwell, Turkey pattern.

similar clasped hands and has the same inscription, but the owner would not have been as wealthy a person.

The rest of the rings were also copper alloy, with the exception of a silver one that was broken. This was a real shame; only a small part remained with a couple of legible letters on it. The plough is bittersweet; it not only destroys coins and artefacts but also it brings up treasure from the depths of the earth. I absolutely have a love/hate relationship with the plough!

Brooches are the next lot of finds from this great site in Fife. Six brooches were found, and six individual brooch pins. The brooch at the top centre was a silver one and the rest were copper alloy. The silver brooch was small by scale, measuring 10mm in diameter; this is about the same size as a hammered silver penny, and affordable for the 'normal peasant'.

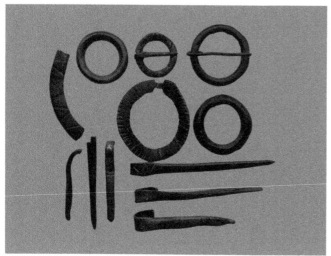

Six scabbard chapes were also found on this settlement; again, these were all made from copper alloy. These were attached to the bottom of a leather scabbard that would have held knives to stop the

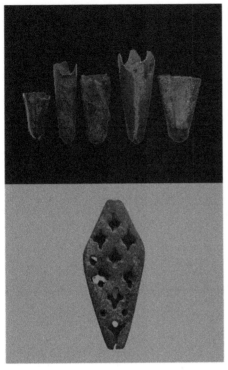

blade end from drawing blood whilst being carried around. You can see the centre chape has a nice chevron design, and the lone chape has eight open worked quatrefoils.

The next find is a little copper alloy hunting dog swivel. These were used to attach the dogs to the collars and leashes. This find shows evidence of hunting near the settlement, and the artefact still moves at the swivel join which is amazing.

The next two finds go hand in hand. One is a medieval padlock, and the other a key—both are copper alloy. The key was designed for

a different lock, which is unfortunate, but the padlock is complete and in good condition. When encountering the padlock, the signal tone was high on my detector due to the thickness of the artefact. It's worth noting again every metal detector or program on a detector

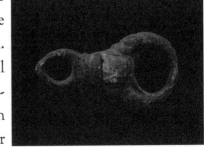

is different; on one of my old metal detectors, it would have been the opposite and I'd likely have had a lower tone.

A lovely little set of copper alloy weighing scales were also found, suggesting the possibility of trade happening on this site.

Similarly, jettons were widely used as counters in the medieval world. These jettons would have aided the merchants with their calculations. My father unearthed this artefact, shown on the opposite page, and again it is copper alloy. It is a French Jetton, and the obverse has a cool im‐ age: it's a bowed dolphin. This dates

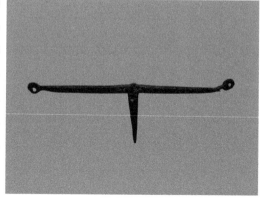

to around the 14th century AD in nice condition this jetton very pleasing.

This next group of artefacts are medieval miscellaneous objects. They are all 100% medieval in style and range from a copper alloy lace chape to protect lace material from fraying (far left) to a copper alloy object (bottom of the picture) that has broken. Two parts were found —a shame it's been damaged by the plough—with chevron decoration going around the top rim and a heraldic shield with one star in each of the four quarters—a lovely find. A wee lead cross (in the bottom right), copper alloy nails, and various other medieval oddities.

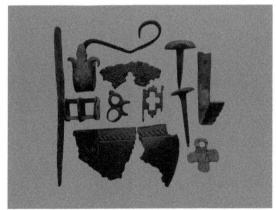

This next find, shown overleaf, is a later medieval copper alloy mount. Part of the Treasure Trove report written by Ella Paul (CO.TT. 49/19) that was used to describe this mount is as follows: 'The object is round in plan and has an integral rounded pin with a fragment of copper-alloy sheet attached to the reverse. The flan has a slight curvature to it. The front face features heraldic decoration. A rounded shield with flat top bears three bendlets sinister (or three thin diagonal lines rising up from left to right) on a background of miniature roundels (pellets). The shield is encircled by tendril-like decoration and a pelleted border. There are small traces of gilding. 26.5mm diameter, 7.2g' (Ella Paul CO.TT. 49/19).

That's all the non-coin artefacts found to date. I'm now going to move on to the coins themselves which were found on this amazing site. There were a great many medieval coins found dating from AD 1153 to AD 1466—a total of 179 hammered coins. I will start with the English coins, then move on to the Scottish coin finds.

The earliest English coins that came from this settlement were two of Henry II (reigned AD 1154–1189). These are early coins from his reign called 'Tealby pennies'. Both are silver, and on the obverse side is a crowned bust with a hand holding a scep-tre. Both sides have a Latin leg-end and beaded borders. On the reverse side is a short-voided

cross pattee with a small cross pattee with a small cross pattee saltire in each angle.

This next group of silver hammered coins are of Henry III (reigned AD 1216–1272). 32 were found in total, ranging from voided short cross pennies, struck in the earlier part of his reign, to voided long cross pennies. Some of the

coins were cut into quarters and halves. They did this to obtain small change, as no other smaller denomination was available at that time. In fact, out of the 32, 23 were half cuts, and this is a good example to show how common the practice was.

Now, on to the largest, most common coin kingship found on site. This is the famous Longshanks himself: King Edward I (reigned AD 1272–1307). He was a tall man; it was his long legs that earned him the name of Longshanks.

This was a period in which this settlement must have been at its zenith. Out of the 69 silver Edward I hammered coins, a few of which were of Edward II (reigned AD 1307–1327), 4 were halfpennies and one was a tiny farthing. This is a period when the coinage changed. Instead of cutting coins, they produced four types of coins: a groat worth 4 pennies, weighing around 5–5.5 grams; a penny weighing around 1.2–1.4 grams; a half penny weighing around 0.6–0.8 grams; and a farthing weighing in at about 0.2–0.4 grams. The farthings are so small, you must be walking slowly to find them with the detector coil right to the ground. Again, the conditions need to be right; there's no point trying to detect these in high grass or stubble fields.

There were various coin mints found amongst the 69 coins. The most common was the London mint, followed by the Canterbury mint, and then the Durham mint. The sheer volume of these coins is a good indication of the vast amount of activity happening during this period in history on this site. All the coins found were spread out over a huge area of the settlement, and therefore not classified as a hoard. For finds to be classified as a hoard, the

objects have to be found within close proximity of each other.

The next few coins are of Edward III (reigned AD 1327–1377). Four silver hammered coins were found: one penny and three halfpennies. There is a significant drop off compared to the Edward

I/II coins. This, in my opinion, was firstly kicked off with the Scottish Wars of Independence, which ran from the late 13th century AD and lasted well into the 14th century AD. A lot of men from Fife went into battle from various villages and never came back. Secondly, the country was hit with severe droughts and floods throughout the same period, causing the crops to fail. Then there was one of the biggest disasters in history with the Black Death arriving in Scotland in AD 1350, killing around one third of the population. All of this ties in with the coinage on the site. This would have been a terrible time for the occupants of this village, as if life wasn't hard enough. After Edward III no other English medieval coins were found by us, but some Scottish coinage went on until around AD 1466 onsite.

Now moving on to my favourite coinage of all: Scottish medieval hammered coins! These vary in detail from the English medieval coins. The most noticeable difference being the reverse with some having stars or pierced mullets on the later medieval Scottish coinage. I prefer to call them stars instead of mullets. Furthermore, the majority of English medieval coins on the obverse have front facing gothic faces, whereas most medieval Scottish coins have side profile portraits with the odd front facing portrait. In general, Scottish coins are also harder to find. Out of all the coins found on site, about 1 in 7 were Scottish coins, excluding the hoard of James III coins I'm going to talk about later. Today, Scottish medieval hammered coins

from the 12th–15th century AD generally tend to fetch more money than most English hammered coins of the same period. The earliest Scottish coin I found was of Malcolm IV (reigned AD 1153–1165). It was a cut silver farthing weighing in at 0.3 grams. The signal for this was tiny. I remember unearthing this one out of the ground and thinking 'that's different.' It's mega-rare, as hardly any Malcolm IV coinage has been found in Scotland. There are only a handful of farthings of Malcolm IV known. I was extremely pleased with this coin.

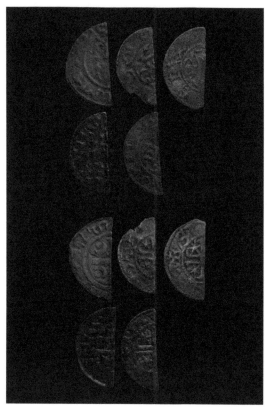

The next group of hammered coins I'm going to talk about are those of William the Lion, King of Scotland from AD 1165–1214. Five half cut silver hammered coins were found. One is an earlier Scottish hammered coin depicting the pellet and crescent type. You can see this in the adjacent picture. The other four are voided short cross coins; you can see the stars on the reverse of these four, signalling they are Scottish coins.

Four nice silver hammered coins of Alexander III of Scotland were also found on this amazing site. Alexander III of Scotland was king from AD 1249–1286. He tragically lost his life on 19th March 1286 when he was travelling from Edinburgh to the little village of Kinghorn in Fife to meet his queen. There is a permanent monument to mark the spot, which is believed to be where Alexander fell to his death near Kinghorn. It's a lovely wee monument by the coast, and worth a visit if you're in the area. Out of the four

coins found on this site, three were early voided long cross coins. One penny and two half cuts. The fourth coin was a penny of the later second issue long cross. The second issue coin inscription reads, obverse: 'ALEXANDER DEI GRA' plain cross; this Latin inscription translates as: 'Alexander, by the Grace of God.' The rest of the obverse has a crowned head to the left with a sceptre. The Reverse reads: 'REX / SCO / TOR / VM' plain cross; this means 'King of Scots' in Latin. The rest of the reverse has a single long cross with pierced mullets (stars) of six points in the angles.

This next Scottish King is my favourite! King John Baliol (reigned AD 1292–1296). My belief is that John Baliol was unfairly treated in Scottish history. In my opinion, he didn't have the full support of the people/nobles at the time, but I'm sure if he had been king for long enough after 'the Sack of Berwick' (AD 1296) and during the long, drawn-out Scottish Wars of Independence that followed, he, like Robert Bruce, would have had a vast army with the support of his people/nobles full of resentment. John's coinage of pennies, halfpence, and the farthing (most importantly the farthing, as I will talk about shortly) were mostly struck at the mint of Berwick. Just before my 40th birthday—I remember it well—I was out detecting. After about 10 minutes I got a signal, but it was scratchy. I don't know why I chose to dig there, because usually these tones detect something iron. As it turned out, I ended up with a horseshoe!

About 6 feet away from the horseshoe I then got a tiny signal on my machine. I only dug about 2 inches down, and out popped a very small grey disc-shaped object. I thought, 'Right, I've got a small pewter button or a hammered coin.' I rubbed it a little with a finger and slowly uncovered the stars (pierced mullets)! My heart skipped a beat, and I knew straight away from the size of the coin and upon discovery of the stars it had to be a Scottish silver farthing. Most Scottish farthings are rare to extremely rare, and therefore very difficult to find. I looked at the bust and I knew it wasn't Alexander III. My next guess was then, maybe it was a Bruce. I got home and, under closer examination, I could see the Latin text on the obverse: 'I[O]hANNES[..]A.' I thought it had to be John Baliol!

It was an amazing moment, such an extraordinary, rare coin! Part of the Treasure Trove report written by Emily Freeman (CO.TT. 242/19) that was used to describe this Baliol farthing is as follows: 'A farthing of John Baliol, second smooth issue. The reverse die is unknown and the obverse die possibly unknown; due to the wear on the coin it is difficult to determine whether the obverse is a previously unrecorded die type. Obv. I[O]HANNES[...]A, bust l., very worn Rev. REX SCO/TO[....], five-pointed mullet in each angle. The only other known example of a second issue farthing for John Baliol was found [in] Suffolk in 1997 which is in the Stewartby collection. 12.00mm, 0.35g' (Emily Freeman CO.TT. 242/19). It was an extremely proud moment for me. This report means it was the first John Baliol farthing to be found in Scottish soil. I received an *ex-gratia* award from the Treasure Trove for this find and split it equally with the landowner. I have kept the horseshoe; it is now in my garden.

Just when you would think there is no beating this, my next find did just that! I heard that one of the 'good fields' had just been ploughed. I decided, for some bizarre reason, to go detecting after my work... and I had just finished a 12-hour night shift! My dad picked me up straight from work and I had a sleep in his car on the way up. I started detecting and I was going slow, mostly due to my zombie-like state! It was just as well, because I caught a tiny signal around about an hour in. I may have missed this if I hadn't been walking literally like a zombie. Another very small grey disc popped out! I wiped it and could see stars. 'YES!' I thought; another Scottish silver farthing. I could read the Latin inscription; this time it was 'IOhANNES.' I couldn't believe it! Another John Baliol farthing. Part of the Treasure Trove report written by Carl Savage (CO.TT. 274/22) that was used to describe this Baliol farthing is as follows: 'A silver hammered farthing of John Baliol (1292-6), first "rough" issue, mint: presumed to be Berwick. Minor wear, slightly chipped. Obverse: crowned bust facing left, sceptre in front, legend is +IOhANNES[...]EIG Reverse: single long cross, six-pointed mullet in each angle, legend is RSC/OT/OR/VN, with the letter N doubled-barred. Diameter: 12.5mm, weight: 0.26g, die axis: 300 degrees. This is the first recorded farthing belonging to the John Baliol's first "rough" issue and so, represents a new type and denomination for this issue.' There is a reference used by the author in this report; it is as follows: Holmes, N.M.McQ. 2020, "New types and other rare examples of Scottish fractions for John Baliol and Robert Bruce", British

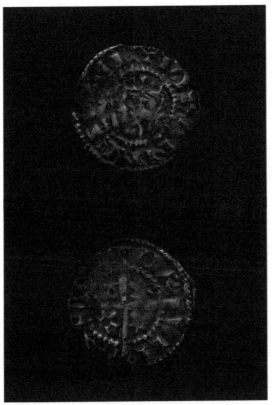

Numismatic Journal, 90, pp. 212–14 (Carl Savage CO.TT. 274/22). A first issue farthing from the early part of his reign! Until now, numismatists thought that only pennies and halfpennies existed of the first issue coinage! This was the first one to be recorded. This find has changed a piece of history! I was lost for words; this Baliol farthing was even rarer than the other one.

After all the research, time, and labour that's gone into this site, I feel like I have a deep connection to this king! I have an immense feeling of pride to have found these two exceptionally rare coins. I have changed the history of numismatics for this king. One man and his metal detector! This is one of the true rewards from this hobby. Two other silver hammered coins of Baliol were found on this site. Both were fairly common halfpennies and were not in the greatest condition—more so on the obverse, with the bust being a bit weak. However, they were fairly decent on reverse—a very welcome addition to my finds on this site.

The next king for me is also special, because my father and I found a hoard of coins from his reign—even though it's my hoard, because I found the first one (a common rule for finding hoards). The hoard is of King James III (reigned AD 1460–1488). He was crowned king after the death of his father, King James II of Scotland. At the siege of Roxburgh Castle, James II was standing too close to one of his own cannons and suffered an injury when it exploded, subsequently bleeding to death. His son, James III, himself died at the Battle of Sauchieburn in 1488.

My father and I were out detecting, and I got a small signal from my detector. I unearthed it and could see it was a green copper hammered coin. I knew it was a James III farthing, as I had seen them before. I started to get more small signals and shouted to my dad to come over. We proceeded to take out 51 of these copper coins over a few weeks. It was like a tap of coins, just flowing from the ground!

These coins were mostly in good condition, and very rare. You can imagine the frenzy of excitement my father and I had in exhuming each one! These farthings are also known as 'Black Money'. They were all type 1, which is the earliest type of copper farthing for James III. The obverse side of the coin displays a crown, and the reverse side displays a saltire cross with smaller saltires at each side. These coins were minted in Edinburgh around AD 1466. This dictates there was a tight chronology for the hoard, with an added pleasure of around 3 billon pennies of James II and a contemporary continental obole mixed in with the farthings.

This is one of the rarest Scottish coin hoards of all time. I was informed, by one of the experts at the National Museum of Scotland, Nicholas Holmes, that 'the last similar hoard was discovered over 100 years ago in Scotland at the 13th century Crossraguel Abbey in Ayrshire. In 1919 some coins of the type you found in your hoard, i.e. type 1 James III black money farthings were mixed in with other coins of similar date in the drain of the abbey latrine' (personal communication, September 15, 2022). You could imagine, maybe, a monk going to the toilet and his wee purse of coins going down the latrine by accident. Yet again, this hoard will change the history of numismatics for a coin issue, another great find of importance! The coins that we found are also

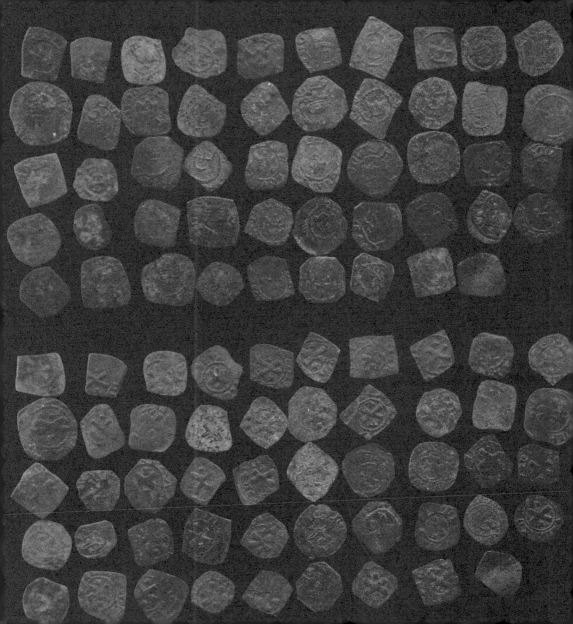

in far better condition than the ones found at Crossraguel Abbey, aiding in the expert's knowledge of the coinage.

Finally, but by no means least, we also found three silver continental sterling imitation coins. Mostly these types of coins were made in Flanders. These are a different type of coinage compared to the typical English Edwardian medieval penny; most didn't have a crown on the gothic face and had different inscriptions.

The centre coin in the picture overleaf is in the best condition out of the three. It is a sterling of Guy of Dampierre; between AD 1251–1305, he was the Count of Flanders. In his later life, Guy was a prisoner of the French during the famous historical event, the Battle of the Golden Spurs (AD 1302). The obverse of what I can make out reads +G:[...]S:FLANDIE with gothic bust wearing roses on the head instead of the traditional crown. The reverse: SIG/NVM/CRV/C[..] long cross with three pellets in each angle.

This site is of national importance due to the rarities discovered. When you break it down, the site itself is rare! To discover a site that's been abandoned and forgotten about over time, with the soil keeping all of the artefacts in great condition for future research, is an anomaly. I would love to see what this site looked like in the past, and what people's daily life was like in this settlement. What did their houses look like, and what was the settlement layout in general? The date range is impressive from 1500 BC to AD 1466, showing the continuous occupation. Some of the artefacts are unique, and others are highly unusual in the numbers appearing—especially to get so many from a particular period, for example, the early medieval ringed pins.

It is not just the ringed pins. As a whole, the sheer abundance and condition of the artefact collection makes it one of the finest Scotland has ever seen! The artefacts and the coinage make this site important. These finds have changed the history of numismatics for the coinage of John Baliol and James III, adding some of the rarest coinage that has ever been found in Scotland. The rare Malcolm IV farthing, and the only two John Baliol farthings to be found in Scotland—one that's entirely unique—not forgetting one of the scarcest Scottish coin hoards of all time, the James III black money farthing hoard of AD 1466: 51 farthings, a once in a century find. All the memories shared on this incredible site will be forever etched in my memory. As I

mentioned before, I'm glad we have put this site on the map for Scottish history. It was in our hands to do so, and that's what this hobby is all about.

It is more than a hobby for me; it's a way of life to be discovered and adds to our knowledge of the past. I'm sure all these souls originating from this site will be patting us on the back, proud that we have shared their history on how they lived and died there. So, I say cheers to all you folk, and thanks for dropping stuff in the ground for us to find!

They were very protective of their money; they were not careless. If you break it down, only 179 medieval coins were found dating from 1153 to 1466. Over a period of 313 years, roughly one hammered coin was dropped every two years. Anybody who says our ancestors were careless with coins is very much mistaken. Roughly a penny was a day's pay in medieval Scotland for these folk, so they would have been very careful with their money. The site coinage finds proves this.

Most of the assemblage from this site is still going through the Treasure Trove system. It will be interesting to see how the story develops after they have studied everything and put a collective interpretation on this site. Other finds from this site include lots of little pieces of tin strewn throughout a vast area along with copper slag, suggesting the people here were possibly making metal objects onsite. The tiny bits of tin were rather annoying, as they are the same tone and size as silver farthings, giving way to false excitement each time!

The permission sites, which we are fortunate to have had, had several areas of interest to us that have produced treasure after treasure. On one of the pastured fields elsewhere, we discovered there used to be an old medieval moated castle and chapel. There are spectacular views on this part of the permission.

The castle and chapel were situated on a piece of land that sat at a higher altitude, giving the old residents there a view for miles around and looking on to the sea below them. This is a great place to put a castle for defensive reasons, giving those occupying the site the advantage of seeing their enemies from a distance. Unfortunately, today there is no trace of the castle or chapel to view on the ground. There is, however, a slight circular ditch where the moat would have once been, stretched around the castle; from an aerial view you can spot some crop markings of where the chapel would have been. The castle was built close to the chapel, which suggests it would have been used as a private chapel for the great wealthy people of the castle.

My father and I gridded this field out with canes to divide the land into small boxes. Laying out smaller pockets of land like this is a great way to detect pasture fields. It prevents any confusion as to what area you have or have not covered with your detector. Splitting out your field this way is very effective in also ensuring fewer signals are missed, but it is hard work moving the canes frequently up and down the field.

Using this method on the location of the castle site, my father and I were able to uncover five medieval finds. This is an average number of finds situated by a medium-sized castle site. The villages generally produce higher volumes of finds due to the increased population size and the daily activities happening within them.

The first discovery we made was a very interesting medieval artefact. It is a medieval anthropomorphic mount, which basically, is an object that has human characteristics. The appearance is intended to represent a saint or an apostle. This nice mount could have been used as a decoration piece to adorn the surfaces of processional crosses or caskets. It would have been enamelled but the soil has not been kind to the copper surface, leaving no traces of such splendour. It was found nearer to the chapel than the castle, as were the other four medieval finds of silver hammered coins. One of the hammered coins is Scottish and is a coin of King William 'The Lion' (reigned AD 1165–1214). This coin is a lovely little half cut coin. The next three hammered coins are English. The first is a silver short cross coin of King Richard I, known as Richard

'The Lion Heart' (reigned AD 1189–1199). He was known as this because of his reputation as a great military leader and warrior.

The next silver hammered coin is a penny of King Edward I (reigned AD 1272–1307). The final silver hammered coin was minted a bit later than the first three and is a silver groat of King Henry VI. He reigned as king during two separate periods in history. The first period of his reign was AD 1422–1461, and the second was AD 1470–1471. This was due to the War of the Roses, where the kingship of England was disputed between the houses of York and Lancaster. This coin was minted in the Calais mint, France. It is easy to see that the coin has also suffered from being clipped during a period when silver was cut off coins to be melted down for extra profit. This coin was around 1 gram underweight due to this.

The finds I have described in this book cover my life as a metal detectorist to date, but I hope there will be many happy years making new discoveries still to come. With luck, this book will have inspired you to find out more about the hidden cultural history that can exist just below our feet.

Image Credits

The illustrations in this book are sourced from the personal photographic collection of the author, with the exception of the following image which is detailed below:

Page 19
Side profile view of terret ring (top image) is Copyright © Falkirk Museums, all rights reserved, and is reproduced by kind permission of the copyright holder.

Treasure Trove Acknowledgements

Text from some of the following Treasure Trove reports were used in this book for the provision of facts. Note that some of the artefacts/coins at the time of writing this book were still going through the Treasure Trove process and do not have Treasure Trove reports yet, and some reports had unknown authors so were not mentioned or used, as far as I am aware. Here is a list:

- **Iron Age tankard handle:** Treasure Trove report (CO.TT. 100/14), unused report written by Dr. Fraser Hunter (pages 14–17).
- **Iron Age linch pin:** Treasure Trove report (CO.TT. 144/17), unused report written by Dr. Fraser Hunter (page 22).
- **Medieval Papal bulla:** Part of the Treasure Trove report (CO.TT. 101/14), used report written by Stuart Campbell pages (pages 26–27).
- **Bronze Age flanged axehead:** Part of the Treasure Trove report (CO.TT. 146/13), used report written by Dr Natasha Ferguson (pages 27–29).
- **Post medieval toy hammer:** Treasure Trove report (CO.TT. 99/14), unused report written by Stuart Campbell (page 28).
- **Roman copper-alloy handle:** Part of the Treasure Trove report (CO.TT. 90/15), used report written by Dr Fraser Hunter (page 32).
- **Roman scabbard chape:** Part of the Treasure Trove report (CO.TT. 12/16), used report written by Dr Fraser Hunter (pages 32–33).

- **Medieval dove mount:** Part of the Treasure Trove report (CO.TT. 74/17), used report written by Stuart Campbell (page 34–35).
- **Roman copper-alloy openwork enamelled racquet-headed plate brooch:** Part of the Treasure Trove report (CO.TT. 86/18), used report written by Dr Fraser Hunter (page 42).
- **Silver medieval fede ring:** Part of the Treasure Trove report (CO.TT. 130/18), used report written by Emily Freeman (pages 49–53).
- **Copper alloy mounts:** Part of the Treasure Trove report (CO.TT. 49/19), used report written by Ella Paul (pages 57–59).
- **John Baliol second issue farthing:** Part of the Treasure Trove report (CO.TT. 242/19), used report written by Emily Freeman (pages 65–67).
- **John Baliol first issue farthing:** Part of the Treasure Trove report (CO.TT. 274/22), used report written by Carl Savage (pages 68–69).

Acknowledgements

I would like to thank my fiancée, Karen, first and foremost! Over the last 12 years she has looked after the kids and held the fort whilst I disappeared detecting at least once but sometimes twice a week. It was also her idea for me to take up the hobby. It was a much better suggestion than the pub!

I would also like to thank my Dad, also Alan, for getting me started and showing me the ropes of this hobby. Not to forget him doing most of the driving over the years, and for making me a nice breakfast roll and coffee when he picked me up in the mornings. We have shared so many great occasions and memories together over the years. Thanks, Dad.

I would also like to thank the Treasure Trove unit for dealing and processing all my finds over the years, and also to the Falkirk Archaeologist Geoff Bailey for his guidance over the years. I have learned a lot about the history of Falkirk District because of him, especially about the Romans in the area. He has been a wealth of knowledge. Thanks, Geoff.

I would like to thank my work colleagues for listening to me constantly turning almost every conversation into detecting! Thanks, guys.

Finally, I would like to thank Tom and Julie Christie for giving me the opportunity to write this book.

I would recommend this hobby of metal detecting to anyone; it is, honestly, hand on heart, one of the best things I have ever done. I hope my story can be extended in the future and cannot wait to read about all the new finds from my budding detectorists both new and experienced! Keep digging, everyone!

About the Author

Alan Baxter is a laboratory technician and a very successful amateur metal detectorist. He lives in the central belt of Scotland. He has been metal detecting for 12 years, ever since his father, also Alan, showed him the ropes of this hobby. In that time, he and his father have managed to unearth some incredible finds in Scotland dating from the Bronze Age to the post-medieval period; the most notable is an Iron Age hoard found in Falkirk District which apparently stands as 'the most significant metallic find in Falkirk District since 1933' (Falkirk Archaeologist Geoff Bailey, personal communication, December 5, 2023), and finding a huge group of Bronze Age to medieval era artefacts from the same area in Fife. These finds collectively make this one of the most important discoveries in Fife and apparently is 'the biggest mixed metallic assemblage of Bronze Age to medieval finds from one site in the whole of Fife' (Fife Council Archaeologist Douglas Speirs, personal communication, December 9, 2023). He hopes in the future, with a bit of luck and research, to extend his portfolio by unearthing even more fascinating finds.

For details of new and forthcoming books from Extremis
Publishing, including our monthly podcasts, please visit our
official website at:

www.extremispublishing.com

or follow us on social media at:

www.facebook.com/extremispublishing

www.linkedin.com/company/extremis-publishing-ltd-/

9 781739 484545